DOLLY DINGLE of DINGLE DELL

BY Grace G. Drayton

Party Dress

Hair Ribbon

Hair-Ribbon

Bend on dotted Lines

Afternoon Dress

Dolly Dingle

Milk-Maid Costume

Gypsey-Jane.

Every Day Dress

Rompers

Cut on dotted Line

Cut on dotted Line

Cut on dotted Line

Cut on dotted Line

Best Day-Day Suit

Party Dress

Gypsey-Jane's Day Day Suit

Roller-Skating Dress

BILLIE BUMPS OF DINGLE DELL

Drawn by Grace G. Drayton

Extra head for Billie Bumps Doll

Billie Bumps

Extra head for Billie Bumps Doll

Robert Roll-Round

Cut on Dotted Line

Rough-Rider's Suit

Rompers

Party Suit

White Mousies

Cut on Dotted Line

Cut on Dotted Line

Foot-Ball Suit

After-noon Suit.

"Toodles"

Sailor Suit

KITTY-CUTIE OF DINGLE DELL

Third of the Dolly Dingle Cut-Out Series

Drawn by Grace G. Drayton

Extra Head

Kitty-Cutie's Supper

Mousie-Pousie

Kitty-Cutie

Extra Head

Bouquet

Duck-a-Luck

Cut on dotted Line

Play-Dress

Cut on dotted Line

Winter Day-Day Suit.

For a Morning-Walk

Trace cradle on white paper. Glue edges on Back all way around Cut on dotted Line.

Cut out center along dotted Line

Cut on dotted Line

A Rainy-Day Suit

Hair-Ribbon

Party-Frock

Afternoon Dress

Dolly Dingle's Trip Around the World

By Grace G. Drayton

G.G. Drayton

CHERRY BLOSSOM

CHERRY BLOSSOM'S FAN.

"PEEK" DOLLY'S JAP DOGGIE

WIG FOR JAPANESE COSTUME

CHERRY BLOSSOM'S KIMONA

CUT ON DOTTED LINE

AFTERNOON DRESS.

TRAVELLING COAT.

Dolly Dingle's Trip around the World

DOLLY VISITS THE HOME OF THE MANDARINS

By Grace G. Drayton

CHIN CHIN CHINAMAN

CHINESE DOLL'S HOUSE

CHINESE PRINCESS COSTUME

PUT A LITTLE BEES WAX ON BACK OF THIS CHINESE WIG AND HEAD-DRES: AND STICK TO DOLLY'S HAIR

BOWL OF RICE WITH CHOP-STICKS

DOLLY'S CHINESE CHOW PUPPY "CHINKIE"

CHINESE FAIRY TALES

G.G. Drayton

DOLLY DINGLE'S TRIP AROUND THE WORLD

Dolly   Visits the Palace   of the Grand Moguls

By GRACE G. DRAYTON

PRINCE DALIM KUMAR'S TURBAN

CUT. CUT THIS WHITE SPACE VERY CAREFULLY

INDIAN TOY ELEPHANT.

DOLLY DINGLE

PRINCE DALIM KUMAR

G. G. DRAYTON

DOLLY'S INDIAN PRINCESS COSTUME.

PRINCE DALIM KUMAR'S COSTUME.

CUT HAT ON DOTTED LINE

FOLK-TALES OF BENGAL

DOLLY DINGLE'S TRIP AROUND THE WORLD

DOLLY VISITS THE LAND OF THE PHARAOHS

By GRACE G. DRAYTON

CUT OUT WHITE SPACES

DOLLY'S AFTERNOON COSTUME

DOLLY'S EGYPTIAN COSTUME

TOY.

JEWEL BOX

TOY CAMEL

AMUL'S ROBE

AMUL HASSEIN
DOLLY'S LITTLE EGYPTIAN PLAYMATE

AMUL HASSEIN'S TURBAN.

G. G. DRAYTON

DOLLY DINGLE'S TRIP AROUND THE WORLD

This Month Your Little Playmate
Visits Sunny Italy

By Grace G. Drayton

Dolly's
Italian
Costume

Dolly's
Toy Donkey.

Dolly's Dress,
And Hat Filled
With Flowers

Dolly
Dingle

Beppo's
Guitar.

Dolly's
Head-
Dress

Beppo-
Dolly's Little
Italian
Playmate

Beppo's
Hat

DOLLY DINGLE'S TRIP AROUND THE WORLD

By Grace G. Drayton

This Month Dolly Picks Edelweiss in the Tyrol

DOLLY'S TYROLEAN HAT

DOLLY'S TYROLEAN COSTUME.

DOLLY'S BEST DRESS

CUT ON DOTTED LINE SO TASSEL WILL HANG DOWN

DOLLY DINGLE— G.G. DRAYTON.

HANS'S MOUNTAIN CLIMBING SUIT.

HANS'S HAT

"HANS." DOLLY'S TYROLEAN PLAYMATE.

A LITTLE DUMB FRIEND

DOLLY DINGLE'S TRIP AROUND THE WORLD

This Month Dolly Visits the Spanish Dons

By Grace G. Drayton

G.G.Drayton

Dolly's Spanish Costume.

Don Juan's Hat— Cut on Dotted Line.

Dolly Dingle

Dolly's Afternoon Costume.

Dolly's Spanish Mantilla cut on dotted line.

Little Don Juan Dolly's Spanish Play-Mate

Don Juan's Bull-Fighting Jacket.

Dolly's Hat— Cut on Dotted Line.

DOLLY DINGLE'S TRIP AROUND THE WORLD

Dolly Doing Her Bit "Somewhere in France"

By Grace G. Drayton

DOLLY'S ALSATIAN HEAD DRESS CUT ON WHITE DOTTED LINE

DOLLY DINGLE

G.G. DRAYTON.

FRENCH DOLL SUZETTE.

DOLLY'S RED CROSS NURSE'S COSTUME.

CUT ON DOTTED LINE ACROSS AND DOWN CENTER

DOLLY'S PARTY DRESS

CUT THE DOTTED LINE FROM ARROW TO ARROW ON HAIR RIBBON

LITTLE FRENCH ZOUAVE PLAYMATE.

DOLLY'S ALSATIAN COSTUME

SUZETTE'S HAT AND DRESS —

DOLLY DINGLE'S TRIP AROUND THE WORLD

Dolly Picks Tulips by the Zuider Zee

By Grace G. Drayton

Dolly's Dutch Costume

Dutch Dollie Katrinka—

G.G. Drayton

Dolly's Dutch Cap.

Dolly's Dutch Cap.

Hansie— Dolly's Little Holland Chum—

Dolly's Sunday Dress

Dolly's Hat

Dutch Dollie for Wagon

Cut Wagon on Dotted Line—

DOLLY DINGLE'S TRIP AROUND THE WORLD

This Month Dolly Visits the
Land o' the Heather

By Grace G. Drayton

G.G. Drayton.

Dolly's Shoes for Scotch Costume.

Dolly's Scotch Costume.

Bobbie Burns Dolly's Pet Duck.

Dolly's Scotch Bonnet.

Dolly's Hat—Cut on Dotted Line—

Highland Mary's Doll "Annie Laurie."

Sandy MacGregor. Dolly's Wee Scotch Doggie.

Little Highland Mary

Highland Mary's Dress and Plaidie

Dolly's Dress.

DOLLY DINGLE'S TRIP AROUND THE WORLD

This Month Dolly Kisses the Blarney Stone   By Grace G. Drayton

KITTY MAVOURNEEN.

CUT OUT

DOILY—

G.G.Drayton.

PEGGY'S DRESS—

DOILY'S IRISH COSTUME

PEGGY'S COSTUME—

CUT OUT

DOILY'S SUNDAY DRESS

DOILY'S SUNDAY HAT
CUT ON DOTTED LINE

PEGGY—
THE LITTLE
IRISH
COLLEEN.

DOLLY DINGLE BACK HOME AGAIN

G.G. Drayton.

ALICE · ALICE

LADY ALICE'S DRESS

LADY ALICE'S BED. CUT ON DOTTED LINE AT PILLOWS. CUT A PIECE OF PAPER TO OUTLINE OF BED AND GLUE EDGES ON BACK OF PICTURE

LADY ALICE.

Dear Santa Claus Please bring me a dolly and of furniture

LADY ALICES HAT. CUT ON DOTTED LINE.

LADY ALICE'S NIGHT GOWN

LADY ALICES STREET SUIT.

CUT ON DOTTED LINE.

LADY ALICE'S PARTY DRESS.

DOLLY'S NEW COAT AND FURS.

DOLLY'S DRESS FOR CHRISTMAS DAY

CRADLE FOR WAX BABY DOLL. MAKE BACK AS YOU DO FOR BED.

DOLLY'S CHRISTMAS EVE NIGHT-PANTIES AND HER STOCKING TO HANG UP,

FOR A GOOD AMERICAN CHRISTMAS

By Grace G. Drayton

TOYS FOR GOOD GIRLS AND BOYS

THE STOCKING THAT SANTA CLAUS FILLED.

SANTA CLAUS.

G.G.Drayton.

PASTE CARD-BOARD STAND BACK OF CHRISTMAS TREE—

LITTLE WAX BABY DOll

WOOLLY TOY PUPPY.